HAWAII Travel Guide

Thomas Leon

Hawaii Travel Guide

ISBN-13: 978-1548325770
ISBN-10: 1548325775

First Edition: June 2017
10 9 8 7 6 5 4 3 2 1

Thomas Leon

C O N T E N T S

Introduction

So, you're going to Hawaii? Lucky you! Your friends and family will sure be jealous because you're going to one of the best places on earth.

As a traveler myself, I've been lucky enough to travel to Hawaii, and my goal for this book is to give you all the useful, practical information about Hawaii so you can enjoy your travel to the fullest!

With accurate, up-to-date information, this book will take you along the scenic trails of Hawaii to provide you with the best vacation ever.

From the most luxurious resorts to affordable albeit comfortable inns, you will discover a plethora of stunning places, including those secret gems that are not normally publicized.

Hike with me all the way up to majestic viewpoints where the azure Pacific Ocean will stretch out for miles at your feet.

Experience thrilling waterfalls that plummet spectacularly from 442 feet. Or better yet, discover how to get to the fiercely guarded Blue Room grotto that was pictured as the world-famous 'Fountain of Youth' in the cult movie, Pirates of the Caribbean: On Stranger Tides.

This book, some good hiking shoes and sunscreen are all you need to explore Hawaii in its pristine glory!

With an abundance of scenic beaches and a wonderfully warm tropical climate, it should come as absolutely no surprise that Hawaii is one of the highest-ranked tourist destinations in the world. Featuring a diverse scenery and hidden wonders in just about every corner, Hawaii basically encompasses several volcanic islands that span across an impressive 1,500 miles- which of course, offers you plenty of new places to visit in one vacation.

Boasting a complex culture with Polynesian origins, Hawaii has a delightfully rich culture with local practices, art and culinary skills that will undoubtedly charm its visitors. The practice of Ho'oponopono, for example, is the local practice of forgiveness and reconciliation, which might help explain why the wonderful people of Hawaii are always in such a good mood. Indeed, if there's one thing that struck me on these islands is how exceptionally friendly the locals are: always up for a chat, always ready to point you towards the right direction. A pot-bellied, heavily-mustached truck driver by the name of Auali'I (which, according to him, means noble), even went out of his way to drive me back to my hotel when I missed the last bus of the day.

As an avid traveler, I can say with absolute certainty that very few places actually came close to matching Hawaii in terms of both scenery and hospitality. Dazzling greens sped past the windows whenever I travelled by bus or train but if you want to experience Hawaii in its purest form, ditch the car in favor of long walks in the countryside. If you ask me, there's nothing like the salt-tinged breeze that flutters through your hair as you drink in the sort of sights that you'll definitely not see elsewhere in the world. My Hawaiian vacation was ideal in many ways but what made it extra-special for me was the warmth and hospitality I encountered, especially in Maui.

Along with friendly locals, you will most certainly be awed by how much there is to do in Hawaii: yes, it might be just a stretch of mainland whose lagoons are dotted by neighboring islands, but seasoned and amateur travelers alike will definitely feel like their vacation is far too short- so read on for my list of the best things to do in Hawaii!

Chapter 1: Touch base with the local slangs

If you're a native English speaker, you will be glad to know that English is one of the two official languages on the island. The second is Hawaiian, but locals also often converse in another language known as Pidgin. Unique to the islands, Pidgin is basically a slang that combines words derived from Hawaii's rich culture.

While virtually all locals do speak English, it does pay off to learn a few essential words in the local language before you head off to any foreign country. Yes, we all know about Aloha (which, incidentally, is used as both hi and bye), but there are quite a few additional words that visitors should probably familiarize themselves with before heading to the island.

Here are some of my personal favorites:

Aloha

It does mean both hello and goodbye, but did you know that Aloha is also used to convey various types of positive feelings and intentions? In Hawaii, Alohoa is additionally associated with goodness, kindness, affection and love.

Ono

Delicious food. That's definitely a word to have in your back pocket when asking for restaurant recommendations!

Howzit

Yes, this means exactly what it sounds like, which is, 'How are you'. You may also want to use this word in conjunction with 'Braddah' which (of course) means friend or brother.

Pono

For obvious reasons, be especially careful with the enunciation when using this one and no, you didn't read it wrongly either. In Hawaii, Pono is defined as righteousness, fair or proper so please, don't take it as an insult if someone walks up to you and compliments you on being 'Pono'.

Mahalo

You might see this word quite often on trash cans in Hawaii, but it does not mean trash. Quite on the contrary, Mahalo means 'Thank you.'

Kokua

Assist or help

Chapter 2: The Hawaiian Islands

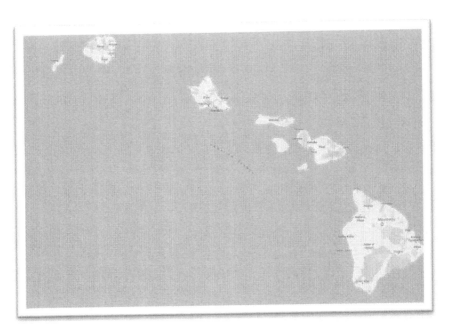

Hawaiian Islands - Google Map

Folks come on- you've already splurged on a trip to Hawaii, so you might as well just go ahead and fork out on short albeit memorable trips to some of the numerous islands that surround the mainland. As out shadowed as they are by Hawaii's many splendors, each island is filled with the kind of wonders that you certainly won't find anywhere else!

The best thing about the Hawaiian Islands? They've literally got something for everyone. And no, I'm not just talking grass skirts and beach barbecues either. Whether you want to check out the bustling city nightlife or simply an isolated retreat by the sea where you can enjoy as much quietness as you want, I have no doubt in my mind that you will find exactly what you're looking for on your Hawaiian vacation.

Maui: Fresh Food and Fun Galore

You just can't leave Hawaii without visiting Maui, which incidentally, happens to be a mere twenty minute's plane ride away from the mainland. Indeed, dotted with artist communities and picturesque towns, Maui is also known as the "Valley of Isle and has been known to attract free spirits from all over the world; eclectic and artsy individuals who fly there especially to soak in that artistic vibe reminiscent of Montmartre.

Along with its versatile eateries, Maui will enthrall you with its majestic beauty and diverse geography: whether you want an adventurous trek through the mountain ranges or simply lounge on the beach as you soak in some much-needed vitamin D, this island does offer something for just about everyone.

Fill up your tummy

Voted "Best Island" by Conde Nast Traveler, Maui is also known for its exquisitely fresh cuisine, courtesy of the firm farm to table policy that lingers on, even in modern times. From freshly grilled lobster on the beach to tequila shrimp or even the world-famous Kalua roast pork, Maui's varied cuisine will certainly please even the fussiest eaters. The best thing about eating in Maui is that you will get to enjoy a diverse blend of the island's heritage, including Filipino-style Adobo dishes, Spanish Pasteles, Portuguese Malasadas and much more.

Enjoy dolphin and whale watching tours

Dolphin and whale watching tours are extremely popular on the island, with most boats departing in the early hours of the morning to optimize your chances of spotting these elusive mammals- yes, it's not exactly pleasant to have to wake up at the crack of dawn when you're on vacation but one look at these majestic creatures and it will all be worth in. In fact, according to Ano- the rotund, gum-chewing guide who steered our boat across Maui's azure waters- these whales have been migrating from North Alaska to the warmer waters surrounding the islands since 1300 AD (at least).

Enjoy your stay at the eclectic Wailea Resort Community

As far as accommodation is concerned, several tourists opt to stay at Wailea Resort community, which is nestled on the southern coast of the island. This community basically consists of a cluster of private homes, B&B's and luxury hotels which you can choose according to your budget. Guests of the resort can also enjoy the pristine stretch of white beaches, shopping, spa, tennis as well as the 18-golf course that once hosted champions in the likes of Tom Watson, Arnold Palmer and Jack Nicklaus.

Lanai: Where Peace and Serenity Reign

When I first landed on Lanai, the first thing that really struck me was the gloriously pure air that was ever so lightly tinged with the sweet scent of pineapples. With a population of less than 4000, this comma-shaped island is ideal for anyone who wants a break from the hustle and bustle that accompanies traditional civilization. Unlike Hawaii and its vibrant and colorful mood, Lanai is quite laidback- mellow almost- with a startling lack of stop lights, traffic jams and shopping malls.

There are hardly any paved roads on the island, so you might want to take a pair of sturdy walking shoes to visit Lanai.

Hike to the highest point of the island

If you feel like unleashing that adventurous bone in your body, don't hesitate to take a trip to Lana'inhale, which is the highest point on the island, standing at over 3,300 feet above sea level. This rain forest offers quite a spectacular view of Lanai, where the deep blue ocean blends seamlessly with the abundant, dark green foliage. With a diverse topography, this forest is also known for its intriguing moon-like rock formations. I would also suggest that you bring along a couple of sweaters when visiting Lanai: after the warmth and humidity of Hawaii, I was completely unprepared for how cool it was on Lanai, especially up on the mountains- which, incidentally, are well worth a trekking adventure.

Check out the different types of accommodation

While Lanai is quite an undeveloped island, it does offer quite a lot in terms of accommodation. Two of the most popular resorts include the Lodge at Koele and the Four Seasons. If you're looking for something cheaper and more laid back, you can also choose from one of the island's many Beds and Breakfasts. These are actually my favorite type of accommodation since they will help you soak in plenty of that unique island culture, without any of the airs and graces that accompany five-star resorts.

Don't forget your helmet!

To get around Lanai, visitors can opt for car rentals, but the best way- at least in my opinion- to visit Lanai is by renting a bicycle. There's nothing like that delectably cool hair whipping through your hair as you feast your eyes on the kind of raw, unvarnished natural beauty of Lanai's desolate landscape.

Molokai: Hawaii's Forgotten Island

Hailed by USA Today as 'Hawaii's Forgotten Island, Molokai (like Lanai) is quite undeveloped and consequently offers a scenic landscape that's still untainted by modernity. 8 miles off the coast of Maui, Molokai is teeming with exotic agricultural crops in the likes of passion fruits, bananas, mangoes and papayas.

Enjoy the benefits of ethical farming

Indeed, these few handfuls of locals who live on Molokai firmly believe in only eating what they grow- which might help explain why this island is reputed for its culinary delicacies. Bear in mind that you won't be greeted with an array of fancy restaurants or food chains over there: in Molokai, food is an art to be savored and appreciated in family-owned inns and B&B's. There are no luxury resorts on the island but you'll certainly find your share of rental cottages and condos.

Check out the unique (and naughty!) rock formations

Getting around Molokai can be quite an exhilarating experience: while you can always rent a car or a spot on a tour bus, more adventurous souls can immerse themselves in the local culture by getting a horse or a mule to cover shorter distances. Contrary to popular belief- and in spite of the visible lack of development on the island-there's quite a lot to do on Molokai. Some of the local attractions can be quite...interesting, to say the least! I doubt I'll ever forget that time when our tour guide announced that we would be visiting the Phallic Rock, which is exactly what it sounds like.

Hike across valleys & take a swim in the waterfall

Alternatively, you might want to take a hike across the Halawa Valley which will take you to a spectacular cluster of waterfalls. This 3-hour hike will take you across a stretch of private land though so you'll undoubtedly need a guide to go through. I would also strongly suggest a pair of waterproof and slip-resistant shoes since you'll pass through a rather thick rainforest on the hike. Don't forget to bring your bathing suit as well since few people can resist the allure of the crystal clear turquoise pool that lie at the feet of the waterfall.

Oahu: Hawaii's own Ibiza!

My first impression of Oahu was that it's basically a playground for adults: there's no denying that this is one island that's teeming with just about any type of watersport you might dream of. From surfing to snorkeling, if you like the water, you certainly need to stop by the island that's been so aptly nicknamed "The Gathering Place" of Hawaii. A bonda fide metropolitan area, Oahu is extremely versatile in the sense that visitors can be as laid-back or active as they want.

Live in the lap of luxury (duh!)

From Michelin-decorated restaurants to world-class golf courses, spas and more, you certainly won't run out of things to do on Oahu. As far as accommodation goes, if you can afford to splurge it's well-worth checking into one of the island's four resort hotels that are brimming with the kind of pampered luxury that one only finds on vacation. Other options include inns, budget hotels as well as rental condos.

And then check out the budget-friendly/free activities

The best thing about Oahu- well, what I liked, at least- is that there are plenty of free or cheap things to do on the island. For example, I attended a surprisingly fun Kuhio Beach Hula show, which is entirely free of charge and will help you soak in quite a lot of island culture. Held on Saturdays, Thursdays and Tuesdays after sunset, these shows also provide excellent platforms for anyone who wants to mingle with the locals. This show includes hula performances, torch lighting ceremonies as well as authentic Hawaiian music (played on locally crafted instruments, no less!) and singing.

Enjoy the unique flora and fauna

In spite of its dense population, Oahu has quite a diverse ecosystem. In fact, you can head over to Laniakea beach on the North of the island where you will find sea turtles teeming in their natural habitats. Just be sure not to try to touch or hold these turtles since they are protected. Because of its crystalline waters, Laniakea beach is also one of Oahu's most picturesque snorkeling spots. If you're feeling particularly bold, you might also want to approach one of the local surf instructors who will take you out to choppier waters where you can experience the thrill of trying to ride a particularly high wave- and failing to, before landing unceremoniously into the water! (As was often the case with me!)

Kuai: A wonderfully charming Metropolitan island

Invigorating and filled with stunning sights, Kuai is the 21st largest island in the USA and is often considered as one of the oldest Hawaiian Islands. With a warm, humid climate not unlike the mainland, Kuai offers plenty of adventures, from kayaking towards the Coconut Coast to boating along the sea cliffs- and more.

Bask in the spirit of Aloha

There's no denying that Kuai is the one island where you can breathe in the Aloha spirit as you walk down the streets: far from resenting the tourist invasion, the locals are actually quite friendly and proud of their heritage.

Immerse yourself in the island's rich history

If you want to learn more about Kuai's multi-layered history, you can check out the Grove Farm Museum or the Kokee Natural History Museum which is found on the West side of the island. Don't hesitate to step out of the carefully structured boundaries of luxury resorts to explore the authentic culture of Kuai as you mingle with the locals and check out one of the island's many eateries.

Feast your eyes on the wonders of the Waimea

Canyon

A trip to Kuai isn't really considered complete without checking out the Waimea Canyon. Nicknamed "The Grand Canyon of the Pacific Ocean", this heritage site stretches across 14 miles and offers breathtaking views of the valley gorges and crags. It also has a lookout point which will literally make you feel as though the vast splendor of the Hawaiian Islands came to rest at your feet.

Chapter 3: Food in Hawaii

If- like me- you happen to be a foodie, well let

me assure you that you will undoubtedly find your own slice of heaven in Hawaii. Forget about fast food chains (as undoubtedly delicious as they might be): this is your chance to explore Hawaiian street food and authentic gourmet restaurants alike. While Hawaii technically belongs to US territory, the cuisine is quite diverse and differs from traditional American food.

It's no secret that Hawaiians love to eat, which might probably explain the wide number of eateries found in virtually every corner of the island. Food in Hawaii is also an excellent way to explore the island's culture and ethnic diversity. Visitors will without doubt be enthralled by the five distinctive types of cuisines through local snacks and dishes in the like of:

- **Shaved Ice:** Okay, it's virtually a crime to go to Hawaii and not try the island's most famous dessert. Shaved ice is available on just about any beach and are served either in dainty plastic cups or cones. These snow cups or cones are drizzled with gloriously sweet and multicolored syrups and are served alongside your choice of ice cream. Some snow cone sellers also add a handful of Azuki beans to accompany your shaved ice.

• **Plate Lunch**: A staple among locals, the famous Hawaiian Plate Lunch consists of a serving of macaroni salad and two scoops of rice served with your choice of side from MahiMahi, Beef Teriyaki, Chicken Katsu, Korean Barbecue and Kulua Pork.

• **Loco Moco**: A nod to Hawaii's American heritage, Loco Moco can be found throughout the islands as well as the mainland. It basically consists of an egg and hamburger steak which is served over rice and usually covered with a generous serving of gravy. According to historians, Café 100- which is a firm favorite among locals- is said to have coined this name.

Restaurant Hopping: One of the best things to do

in Hawaii

Take your taste buds on an adventure of their own as you explore the numerous eateries that helped put Hawaii on the map. Regardless of how much you're willing to spend on food, there'll always be something for you to try in Hawaii, so diverse is its cuisine. Having said that, it's worth checking out at least one gourmet restaurant and even a few street food stalls just to experience the unique medley of flavors that the island is so proud of.

Discover fine Hawaiian cuisine in gourmet restaurants

Gourmet restaurants will allow you to explore Hawaii's culinary landscape with just the right touch of luxury. When I was in Honolulu, I was lucky enough to secure a reservation at Alan Wong's, one of the most well-known gourmet restaurants in the area. Granted, the dishes do have a rather exorbitant price tag attached to them, but then again, it's well-worth it to sample Chef Wong's aromatic mastery. Just be ready to fork out between $80 and $105 per person for a seven-course tasting menu. Some of my favorites include their avocado salsa, chopped ahi sashimi as well as Kalbi-typed grilled short ribs.

If you're visiting Maui, do try to stop by Ko, a unique cross-cultural cuisine found at The Fairmont Kea Lani. This gourmet restaurant offers a fusion of century-old dishes that originated when workers from Portugal, Korea, Philippines, Japan and China arrived in Hawaii. Some of Ko's most popular dishes include Chap Chae- Korean style yam noodles- as well as Portuguese Bean Soup. I was also quite fond of the Lumpia, which is basically a spring roll prepared Filipino-style. Ko is quite a fancy place though, with entrees starting at around $39. However, you certainly won't be disappointed since it offers a highly diverse menu with generous portion sizes.

Street food for a cheap albeit authentic taste

Then again, if you're travelling on a small budget, you might not be all that willing to fork out nearly 40 bucks on a mere entrée. Don't worry though: there's absolutely no doubt that you will be able to enjoy equally delicious meal at a fraction of the cost. Speaking of food, let's not forget that Hawaii can get quite hot and after hours of endless adventures, there's nothing like a gloriously cool lemonade to cool you off. Hawaii in fact specializes in Mason-jar lemonades which you can found in most farmer's markets. Instead of just lemon juice, water and sugar, these irresistible concoctions also incorporate pitaya and pineapple flavors. Throw in an additional 50 cents and the vendor will sprinkle some 'Li Hing' powder' on top for some serious kick.

Poke is another Hawaiian delicacy that can be found both in street food stalls and gourmet restaurants. The best thing about eating Poke on an island surrounded by the sea is that the fish is always fresh. The most popular type of Poke in

Hawaii is made from fresh, ruby-red Ahi, marinated with sesame oil, seaweed, onions, Hawaiian salt as well as shoyu.

If there's one thing Hawaii is known for, it's spam. Therefore, be ready to discover spam cooked in a ways you can't even begin to imagine. For example, Spam Musbi is found in several food trucks and stalls all over Hawaii. This is basically a type of spam-based sushi which is composed of a slice of grilled spam wrapped over a bed of rice and held together with some nori. Best of all? It's far less expensive than real seafood sushi. Variants of Msubi also include roast pork, Portuguese sausage, pork cutlets, chicken teriyaki as well as chicken katsu, instead of spam. Vendors also like to experiment by adding scrambled egg underneath the layer of spam.

Sink your teeth in a ripe, juicy fruit

I'll never forget the simple pleasure of lying on a sun-kissed beach, the wind lapping ever so gently at my face as I nibbled of pieces of delightfully fresh fruit. I don't know if it's the sun or the warmth, but for some reason, Hawaiian fruits tend to be gorgeously sweet and bursting with juice.

Then again, you didn't exactly go to Hawaii to eat pineapple, did you? Of course not. But did you know that Hawaii is also home to some of the most exotic fruits in the world? Examples include Lilikoi, a fragrant type of passion fruit, Breadfruit which is cooked and eaten either with salt or sugar, Cherimoya, which has been known to taste like a mix of pears, strawberries and bananas and the famous Pitaya- also known as Dragon Fruit because of its green and bright pink skin.

One of my favorite things to do in Hawaii is to try as many fruit-based concoctions as I can, such as sweet Tamarind compote and Green Papaya salad.

Chapter 4: Accommodation in Hawaii

True to the world-famous Hawaiian hospitality, you certainly can be sure that you'll find somewhere that matches both your budget and expectations- regardless of whether you're staying on the mainland or on one of the neighboring islands. Because Hawaii depends largely on is tourist industry, absolutely no expense has been spared in creating a plethora of accommodation to comfortably sleep the massive afflux of visitors.

So, whether you want to tighten the belt and go for a cheap B&B or splash out on an ultra-sophisticated resort, just be sure to check out review sites first to avoid any nasty surprises when you land. Considering the number of tourists who visit the island every year, it's also good idea to book your accommodation several weeks in advance. Don't forget that if you book during off-peak seasons, you might snag quite a few deals, including discounts and hotel perks.

Luxury Resorts: Because you deserve to treat yourself

If there's one place where can afford to be indulgent, it's undoubtedly Hawaii. For this reason, Hawaii and its surrounding islands are brimming with an extensive number of luxury resorts that practically ooze charm and elegance. Imagine lounging on your own private beach-front cabana as you watch the sun sink beneath the horizon, sipping on a chilled glass of bubbly brought to you by your own personal butler.

Yep- this is exactly the kind of indulgent lifestyle that you can expect when checking into a luxury Hawaiian hotel. Some of the most popular choices include- but are by no means limited to- the Four Seasons, Ritz-Carlton, Royal Hawaiian, Grand Hyatt Kauai as well as the Lodge at Koele.

Forget reality at the 5-star Grand Wailea Resort (Maui)

A one of a kind hotel, the Grand Wailea Resort is my personal favorite and ideal for anyone who wants to take a well-deserved break from reality. Boasting breathtaking scenery and opulent luxury, this hotel gives you every reason to splurge: from the nine sparkling swimming pools to floating thatch-roof restaurants, this is one resort that shows you what the high life is all about. Brimming with an exceptional variety of amenities and services, the Wailea Resort is a mere half hour away from Kahului airport. Because of its proximity to Honolulu (30 minutes by plane), you can visit mainland Hawaii as often as you'd like to. In fact, most guests choose to drop anchor at the Grand Wailea to escape the hustle and bustle that normally accompanies the mainland.

Suites & Rooms

Guests of the resort can choose between different types of rooms, depending on their budget. If you can afford to splurge, however, don't hesitate to go all out and opt for ones of their 1,950 square feet suites: The Wailea, Napua, Napua Club Royal, Napua Club Nani, Molokini, Honua Ula, Deluxe and the Alii suites will certainly make you feel like a King/Queen for the entire duration of your stay.

If you're travelling on a limited budget, rest

assured you will still have a choice of spacious and elegant garden or ocean facing rooms.

Surrounded by 40 acres of emerald green foliage and tropical landscapes, you can be sure to never run out of things to do as a guest of the Grand Wailea. Here are a few of my personal favorites:

Harmonize your body, mind and spirit at the award-winning Spa Grande

With treatments designed to seamlessly blend ancient Hawaiian, western and eastern traditions, Grand Wailea's Spa Grande offers a unique experience that will re-energize and refresh you as you continue your Hawaiian holiday. From soothing massages to facials, hydrotherapy circuits and many more, this spa even offers family packages with treatments especially designed for teens and children. A beauty salon is also included, where you can enjoy as many manicures and pedicures as you want.

Make the most out of the Beach Club

Guests of the Wailea Resort have exclusive access to the beach club, where you can delight in unlimited use of boogie boards, paddle boards, snorkel equipment and kayaks. The club agents will be all too happy to help you work on your surfing skills if you ask them too. In fact, guests aged 12+ are even entitled to one complimentary scuba diving lesson in the resort's own training pool. More experienced divers can book boats that will take you off the reef where you can feast your eyes on the many hidden wonders that lie beneath the Pacific Ocean.

Work on your swing (and tan!)

A mere two minutes away from the resort is the world-famous Wailea Golf Club which is especially known for its sweeping views of Mount Haleakala and its three perfectly manicured courses. A personal favorite of mine is the Blue Course, which is found on Mount Haleakala's lower slopes. Designed by Arthur Jack Snyder, this course offers a truly spectacular view of the ocean. Best of all, you get to work on your tan and swing at the same time!

Get a slice of culture at the hotel's on-site Napua Art Gallery

Because Grand Wailea Resort is a city in its own, it even has its own on-site art gallery where you can enjoy the glorious fusion between Aloha and Art. From internationally renowned artists to local ones, you will be treated to an enticing showcase of some of Hawaii's finest sculptures, furniture, ceramics and paintings. The Napua art gallery also features the most extended collection of Chihuly glass in the entire Pacific Ocean.

Budget-Friendly Accommodation: Cheap & Chic

While Hawaii is certainly the ideal place to finally relax those purse strings and indulge yourself, rest assured that there are plenty of budget-friendly accommodation that you can choose from- both on the mainland and its surrounding islands. Depending on how much you're willing to spend, you can either go for cheap hotels or motels or even aptly located B&B's that will help you experience the very best that Hawaii has to offer, without necessarily having to break the bank.

If you ask me, budget-friendly establishments are actually the best types of accommodations for the curious traveler since you will be able to fully immerse yourself in the unvarnished Hawaiian culture, without the sheltered golden bubble that most high-end resorts tend to wrap around their guests.

Some of the better-known budget accommodations in Hawaii include, the eco-friendly resort, Waianuhea, Paia Inn Hotel, Pineapple Inn Maui, Shoreline Hotel and the Aston Waimea Plantation Cottages, among others.

One of my personal favorites is the Volcano Forest Retreat, where guests can bask in the beauty of a virgin rainforest during the entire duration of their stay on the big island.

Volcano Rainforest Retreat: Comfort on a budget

If you want to experience Hawaii in its rawest, unvarnished form, you really can't go wrong with the Volcano Rainforest Retreat. I had the privilege of spending a week in this phenomenal B&B and contrary to what you might think, you certainly won't have to compromise on your comfort in spite of the affordable prices.

Located on mainland Hawaii, this Bed & Breakfast is a mere few miles from some of the most magnificent landscapes on the big island. With a casually elegant décor, this B&B also boasts four guest cottages that are beautifully sheltered under a canopy of emerald green leaves. This is undoubtedly the ideal place for anyone who wants to be in tune with the majestic Hawaiian wildland while enjoying the cool breeze rustling through the rainforest. In spite of its affordable price tag, the Volcano Rainforest Retreat does provide a plethora of amenities designed to render your stay even more comfortable.

Rustic accommodations with a hint of luxury

Volcano Rainforest Retreat's guest cottages feature cozy wooden interiors with floor to ceiling windows to provide spectacular views of the forest. Wake up to the soft chirp of birds as you breathe in fresh air that's completely untainted from city pollutions.

Guests can expect to spend around $30 per guest, per night. A few of the numerous amenities include:

- Private fridge

- Free WiFi

- Private deck

- Jacuzzi hot tub

- Private bathroom

- Free breakfast (room service)

Things to do around the Volcano Rainforest Retreat

Explore the neighboring volcanoes

A mere 10 minutes away from the retreat is found one of the most popular tourist spots in Hawaii: the Hawaii Volcanoes National Park, which incidentally is also an International Biosphere Reserve as well as a United Nations World Heritage Site. This park houses the world-famous Kilauea volcano, which according to the locals, is home to the Hawaiian goddess Pele. The volcano park is also the ideal place for tourists who want to explore rainforest and desert trails, lava tubes, steam vents, craters and even petroglyphs.

Best of all, this is the ideal place to spot extremely rare and native birds as well as the centuries-old Ohia trees. If you fancy an adventure, you can also hike your way up to the summit of Mauna Loa.

Experience the wonders of the universe

The Volcano Rainforest Retreat is also quite close to the Mauna Kea Observatories, where visitors can stargaze to their heart's content. This is more than just any regular stargazing experience though since one of the observatories is actually found on Mauna Kea at an altitude of 9000 feet. This provides you with a unique insight of the Hawaiian night sky.

Because this observatory is located at a stunning 13,803 feet above sea level, there are a few health guidelines for visiting this stunning place.

Akaka Falls State Park

A short drive away from the Volcano Rainforest Retreat is found Akaka Falls State Park which is home to two of the most scenic waterfalls in Hawaii. If you're trying to curb your expenses, rest assured that this is one state park that caters to limited budgets, with an entry fee of $5 for cars and $1 if you choose to venture on foot. Along the gentle hike, you will be able to spot draping ferns, bamboo groves, wild orchids and other such natural delights. Of course, it's a good idea to bring along your swimwear since I can practically guarantee that you won't be able to resist the lure of the Akaka Falls- which is also known as the most beautiful waterfall in mainland Hawaii. This waterfalls plummets an incredible 442 feet into a stream, and it's quite a common sight to see visitors frolicking about in its crystalline waters as they cool off after their hike.

Chapter 5: Exploring Hawaii

Hawaiian Island Hopping

Six of the main Hawaiian Islands are open to tourists and unlike what you may think, it is neither costly nor difficult to hop from one island to the other. In fact, four of the main islands offer direct flights to various US states, which means that you don't necessarily need to go through the Hawaiian mainland first. These four islands are Oahu, Kauai, Maui and the mainland itself. It is also possible to book inter-island flights through local airlines such as Mokulele, Island Air, Go! And Hawaiian Airlines. In most cases, you only need around 20-50 minutes to get from one island to the other.

While there are no official ferry transfers per se, you can book private boats to charter you between the different islands. On firm land, you can easily go around by shuttle, car, bus and even bicycles. Rentals normally ask for a valid driving license so be sure to have all your paperwork ready. Service desks are available at most hotels and airports. Major vehicle rental companies include Thrifty, National, Hertz, Dollar, Budget, Avis and Alamo.

Alternatively, taxis are available in just every corner of the islands. I would personally steer clear of hotel transportations since these are notoriously expensive. And if you've got the stamina and you don't mind a little bit of sun, don't hesitate to walk to your destinations. Trust me- the sights in Hawaii are quite unlike anything you will ever see elsewhere. A languorous assault on the senses, the sights in Hawaii are nothing if not spectacular, providing you with plenty of photo opportunities. You know. Should you want to elicit the envy of your friends on social media and all. Just sayin'.

Booking a tour V/S Exploring the Island on your own

If you're visiting Hawaii for the first time, it might be best to book a tour or a guide to show you around in order to avoid losing precious vacation time trying to find your way around the islands. Don't forget that most guides are native to the country so you will undoubtedly be treated to your fair share of anecdotes and legends that you certainly won't find in history books. Guides can also assist you in finding the best deals in terms of restaurants, shopping and the likes.

Still, if you're limited by a shoestring budget, there's no denying that a guide can be quite expensive, as are tours. For this reason, it might be a good idea to do as much research as you can prior to visiting Hawaii in order to explore the island on your own. Don't forget that going around by yourself means having to book your own shuttle or look for your own taxis.

Chapter 6: Fun Things to do in Hawaii

Enjoy the refreshing waters!

The best thing about Hawaii is that come summer or winter, the numerous beaches around the islands maintain a moderately balmy temperature- providing you with the perfect setting for a refreshing dip after a long, adventurous day. I would highly recommend booking a sunset cruise off the coast of Oahu: indeed, there's nothing quite like watching the sun sinking beneath the waves, leeching the sky pink as you sip on a delectably dry, crisp champagne. You can also check out the Mauna Lani Sunset Sail Adventure which will take you on a breathtaking sunset cruise around Kohala, fueled by unlimited cocktails as well as scrumptious Hawaiian Pupus. On this cruise, you will also be able to enjoy a magnificent view of the famous Kohala, Haleakala, Hualala and the Mauna Kea mountains.

Jet skiing is another exhilarating nautical experience that you certainly can't miss if you're visiting Hawaii. Experience the thrill of coursing through the deep blue waters off the coast of Maunalua Bay near Honolulu. If you've never piloted a jet ski before, rest assured they are extremely easy to operate. Solo drivers should be at least 16 years old.

Of course, there's no better way to enjoy a bird's eye view of Hawaii's stunning lagoon than to book a parasailing session. After surfing, parasailing is one of the most sought-after water sport in the big island. A 1.5 hour session can cost you around $60 and the rider must weigh at least 60 pounds. I would personally recommend a parasailing session at Maunalua Bay, where you will be treated to an absolutely thrilling view of Oahu's emerald green and turquoise coastline. Waikiki is another wonderful area to enjoy an exhilarating parasailing session.

And there's plenty to do on land too

If there's one thing you don't want to miss when you're in Hawaii, it's a fun-filled bash on the beach by nightfall. Hawaiians certainly know how to party and you will undoubtedly be enthralled by the extravagant evening beach shows that cater to both tourists and locals alike. In O'ahu, for example, I was invited to the kind of dazzling show that can easily be compared to the likes of

Broadway (or even Las Vegas)! In Waikiki, you can lounge on the beach and enjoy a mouthwatering barbecue as you enjoy dramatic renditions of centuries-old Polynesian stories. If you're lucky, you might even get to attend a show with the famous Hawaiian stage illusionist, John Hirokawa, who will undoubtedly transport you to a whole other world filled with magic and fantasies.

Of course, no trip to Hawaii can be deemed complete without the traditional luau. Don a grass skirt and a lei (flower garland) and sway to the renditions of Rock-A-Hula by a campfire. Most hotels do make it a point to host at least one luau party, complete with local cocktails and grilled delicacies. If you're visiting Waikiki, be sure to check out the island's most famous jazz club, Blue Note. In fact, you might even want to book a dinner cruise onboard the locally-renowned E Sea Rider before finishing off the evening with a night cap on one of the island's many nightclubs.

Fun-filled family activities to entertain the kids

Family time at an interactive center

If you're travelling with your kids, fear not: there's more than enough to do in Hawaii to keep the entire family occupied. The Hawaii Children's Discovery center, for example, is located in Honolulu and- contrary to most museums- offers an interactive environment that actually encourages children to touch their numerous exhibitions. With fun programs such as rotating classes as well as Art in the Park, this center additionally stimulates your child's creative spirit while providing fun and entertainment for the whole family.

Explore the diverse Polynesian culture

Alternatively, you might also want to check out the Polynesian Cultural Centre which can be reached after a picturesque drive across Oahu's North Shore. Boasting 42 acres of stunning greenery, this center is also known for its interactive villages as well as its friendly employees who are always decked in traditional outfits. At the Polynesian Cultural Centre, you will also have a chance of exploring the traditions and cultures of Tahiti, Fiji, Aotearoa, Samoa, Tonga and, of course, Hawaii. Kids will have a chance to participate in Maori games, Tahitian dances, Poi Pounding and Lei Making, among others.

Splash away at the Hawaiian Waters Adventure Park

If there's one thing that will undoubtedly thrill adults and children alike, it's the Hawaiian Waters Adventure Park. This theme park is spread across 25 acres and offers a stunning range of fun-filled water activities such as a tubing river, wave pools or even the kind of water slides that drop seven stories! While the little ones are splashing about (and supervised by the numerous lifeguards), parents can relax and enjoy the café, gift shop, food court, arcade and even a volleyball court. Best of all, the waterpark also has a spa section, complete with refreshing drinks such as cucumber water, pineapple cocktails and whirlpools. The Hawaiian Waters Adventure Park is found around 40 minutes away from Waikiki and you will be able to enjoy amazing views of the shoreline on the way.

Explore gardens and forests on a Segway

Another fun activity that will undoubtedly delight your kids is the Botanical Segway Adventure, where the whole family will be able to explore some of Hawaii's most enchanting gardens as they glide on a Segway PT. If you're a complete beginner, you can opt for the 60-minute Ke Ola Tour which promises to invigorate your senses as you ride among exotic plants that are unique to the island. This tour is quite easy and ideal for families with smaller children.

For a more challenging experience, you can opt for the 120 minutes Hanapueo Tour on the thrilling Segway X2, an off-road vehicle that will provide you with a one-of-a-kind experience. On this particular tour, you will be able to explore the Hanapueo streams as well as a rainforest brimming with various types of rare plants and trees. At the end of the trip, you can add a zip lining extra to your package and experience the toe-curling thrill of gliding above the Kamaee Falls.

Must-try Solo Experiences for single travelers

Solo travelling has undeniably spiked in popularity over the past few years. The best thing about taking a solo trip to Hawaii is that you'll never feel guilty- definitely not on an island bursting with other hyper holiday-makers who are probably just as eager as you to explore everything that Hawaii has to offer.

Golf under the tropical sky

Admittedly enough, I did travel to Hawaii in a group but there were days when we each felt like doing our own thing, which left me with some time on my own. If you ask me, one of the best solo Hawaiian activities is golf: for starters, you really won't find other courses in the world that matches the exquisite scenery, where green blends almost seamlessly into turquoise. One of my favorite courses in Hawaii is the Arnold Palmer which is found in the Turtle Bay Resort, Honolulu. This championship course stands at an elevation of 100 feet from the Pacific Ocean and stretches across five miles of silky beaches. Providing you with a superior view of Kawela beach, this 18-hole course additionally has a front nine that plays just like Scottish Links.

Let the Maui Rain Shower wash your troubles away

In every country that I travel to, I try to book a

spa day on my own to allow my body to recuperate from day after day of exhilarating adventures. There's no denying that Hawaii does provide the ideal setting for a perfect spa day, with invigorating Polynesian treatments and energizing body massages.

One of my favorite spas in Hawaii is the Willow Stream Spa found in Maui. With state-of-the-art features, this particular spa offers treatments based on ancient Hawaiian traditions such as the Experience Shower where you lie on your front and relax as soothing gushes of water stroke your skin from all sides. Visitors can choose from different types of showers such as the Ua Hekili Evening Storm, Ua Naulu Afternoon Rain, Ua Noe Morning Mist as well as the Ua Loku Power. Highly recommended for fatigue and stress, these showers are available for both men and women.

In terms of body massage, I particularly enjoyed the 120-minutes Huaka'i Kupono Hawai'I, which roughly translates to 'Natural Hawaiian Journey'. In true local spirit, a combination of pure stream water, earth deposit, fruits and rich flora is used alongside sea salt is used in a full-body scrub. After the exfoliation, the therapist wraps your body in soothing Ti Leaves and clay, allowing you to relax and drift away while she performs a calming scalp massage with a citrus hair mask. To complete the experience, your body is massaged with a sweet-smelling mélange of coconut body butter and Maui Vanilla Bean, leaving you radiant and re-energized, ready for another Hawaiian adventure!

Seek out those hidden gems

The Hawaiian mainland and its surrounding islands are bursting with hidden gems that are so perfectly concealed that you won't have to push through the crowds or wait in line for hours. Perfect for solo travelers, these beautifully sheltered places will provide you with some much-needed calm and tranquility. One such place is The Blue Room, found on Kauai. This wet cave literally looks like a postcard, something which is only enhanced by the gentle streams of sunlight that play across the crystalline waters. Unfortunately, the fresh-river stream has been declared a no-swimming zone, which might help explain the lack of visitors. Regardless, The Blue Room is an undeniably soothing place. Just to give you a mental image of how absolutely stunning this grotto is: this was the exact cave that was pictured as the "Fountain of Youth" back in Pirates of the Caribbean: On Stranger Tides.

If you're seeking those hidden gems, you might also want to check out the Saltwater Swimming Hole which is found on the mainland. This swimming hole is fed by the gloriously warm Pacific Ocean and also offers an exclusive beach access. While this saltwater pool is found on private property, it's completely free and open to the public.

In my opinion, the best way to seek out Hawaii's many hidden gems is to get friendly with the locals. Hit up the lesser-known pubs, get chatty with the hotel staff and don't hesitate to strike up a conversation with your tour guides since they're aptly placed to direct you towards what will undoubtedly be a one-in-a-lifetime experience.

Top 5 Hawaiian Attractions

Akaka Falls State Park

Located north of Honomu on the Hawaiian mainland, Akaka Falls State Park will take your breath away- yes, it's that stunning. The general air of fairy tale-like enchantment that shrouds this natural wonder is only enhanced by the local folklore: according to an old Hawaiian legend, if a stone from the Akaka is struck by a branch of the Lehua Apane tree, the skies will darken, giving way to a massive rainfall. Folklore or not, there's no denying that exciting air of mystery which greets you as you first venture into the shadows of the gorges, illuminated only by the golden shafts of light that flicker through the green canopies.

At the end of your self-guided trek across the gorges, you will reach a scenic viewpoint which will offer you a panoramic view of the surroundings where you will be able to enjoy the crashing Kahuna Falls in all its majestic glory. Open between 8.30am to 6pm, this state park includes several steps and a paved route, so some stamina is required to complete the trek. Don't miss a chance to look through the giant binoculars that have been set up at the viewpoint to increase your chances of spotting some of the rarest bird species in the world.

Diamond Head State Monument, Oahu

One of the top-rated landmarks in Hawaii, the Diamond Head State Monument is known to locals as Le'ahi, the sister of goddess Pele. The name Diamond Head didn't quite stick until the late 1700's when western settlers were convinced they would unearth diamond at the foot of the summit. Unfortunately, this didn't exactly work out well for them, considering that the so-called diamonds turned out to be Calcite Crystals (which, in case you don't know, are entirely worthless).

Regardless, the name stuck and is nowadays a firm favorite spot among tourists, especially because of its historic hiking trails. Rest assured though that this is no ordinary trail: on your way to the summit, you will be greeted to a striking coastal view which is only enhanced by the kind of refreshing sea air that one can only get at an altitude. This attraction encompasses over no less than 475 acres and this includes both the outer and inner slopes of the crater which gives you a lot of ground to cover. This is why I would personally recommend that you set aside a full day to explore this truly impressive spot. According to historians, this monument was formed around 350,000 years ago after a massive volcanic eruption. Don't forget your hat, sunscreen and plenty of water because this is one challenging hike!

Camp under the stars at the Keaiwa Heiau State Recreation Area

Whether you do this alone or with a group, this is one camping trip that will help you connect with nature. This 384-acre park is located around 12 miles from Waikiki and includes showers, picnic tables and restrooms. Located in the middle of a wonderfully thick rainforest, this state park is also reputed for its ancient eucalyptus and pine trees that will provide some much-needed respite from the Hawaiian sun. 10 campsites are available for tourists from Fridays to Wednesdays and the camping fee is only around $11 per night. I would suggest that you start out early and set up your tent before exploring one (or several) of the beautiful trails that surround the campsites.

For example, the 4.8 miles Aiea Loop Trail both starts and ends right in the Keaiwa Heiau State Recreation Area, offering you unique views of the Diamond Head, Honolulu and even Pearl Harbor. While this hike is not exactly challenging, there are some uphill trails and even a stream crossing so you might need to don a sturdy pair of hiking boots. Be prepared for potentially slippery slopes with exposed roots. After the hike, you can enjoy an invigorating dip in the refreshing stream before setting up camp back at the site. Several barbecue grills have also been set up near the campsite, should you wish to enjoy a delectable Al-Fresco dinner with your friends and family.

Kona Coffee Tours: A one of a lifetime experience

Okay, whether you like coffee or not, do yourself a favor and check out at least one of the Kona Coffee Tours. Easily one of the most entertaining tours I booked on Hawaii, these tours enable you to choose from hundreds of coffee farms on mainland Hawaii. On these tours, your guides will show you around the plantations to see how coffee is grown. Following that, visitors will be taken through the different steps of drying, processing and roasting, following which you will be treated to various types of coffee samples. Most tours also include a visitor center where you will be able to purchase coffee and mugs to take home as souvenirs.

If you ask me, February and March are the best

times to visit coffee plantations in Hawaii since the plants are flowering and believe me when I say you don't want to miss the sight of coffee plantations in full bloom. Generous bunches of white fragrant flowers stretch out for miles, which is why they are locally known as "Kona Snow". Because coffee is such an integral part of Hawaiian history, these plantations often display century-old accessories and equipment.

Touring Pearl Harbor: A must-do in Hawaii

As tragic as the events of Pearl Harbor were, there's no denying that visitors from all over the world flock to this historic site, which still remains an active military base to date. A must-do in Hawaii, a tour of Pearl Harbor is both sober and exhilarating. For security reasons, you won't be allowed to take your bags on any of the sites, but for a fee, visitors can stow any luggage or backpack in a secure storage area.

Because this site receives an afflux of visitors, it

is extremely important to book your tours early. If you're travelling on a restricted budget, you will be glad to learn that both the admission and parking at the Pearl Harbor Visitor center are completely free, as is the admission to the renowned Arizona Memorial. This is the site where you will be able to pay tribute to the 1,177 marines and sailors who died during the attack. The memorial sites rests right above the sunken ship, which means that you'll be transferred there by boat.

Another must-try when you're visiting Pearl Harbor is the Pacific Aviation Museum which is located on Ford Island. Again, this site is reachable by boat. I was quite impressed to see that the museum is found in the original hangar that was attacked so many years ago. On this particular site, you will be able to tour no less than 50 different exhibits including vintage aircrafts. Visitors of the Pacific Aviation Museum are also treated to the award-winning documentary, East Wind, Rain. If you're an adrenaline junkie (like me!), you might want to fork out an additional fee to try some of the best combat flight simulators in Hawaii. A café, museum store and historical videos are also included.

Chapter 7: Shopping in Hawaii: One of the best things to do

Avoiding tourist traps

Because of its diverse culture, shopping in Hawaii is a highly enjoyable experience, especially if you're interested in local artefacts and souvenirs. However, because of the massive tourist industry, this island- like most popular destinations- does come with its share of tourist traps.

Here are a couple of tips to avoid falling into them:

Check out the North Shore

The southern beaches of Hawaii are full of high-end resorts and hotels, so you can certainly expect over-inflated prices. The northern shore, however, is just as stunning but far quieter and most local vendors that I've encountered actually enjoyed haggling. More importantly, shopping on the north shore will treat you to scenic hidden waterfalls, isolated beaches, jungle hikes and lava tubes.

Avoid shopping centers

The majority of shopping centers will only carry the same brand stores that you can find just about anywhere in the world. Besides, the majority of these stores are extremely expensive, thanks to designer accessories and clothes. Your best bet would be to go ditch the luxury malls in favor of smaller towns where you can shop for various types of items that reflect Hawaii's distinctive culture.

Don't be afraid to haggle

A real sucker for bargains, I consider haggling to be something of a sport and luckily enough, street vendors in Hawaii don't mind a bit of bargaining. Markets and fairs sport just about anything from food items to volcanic ash soaps, clothes, souvenirs, sculptures and more.

Where to find the best bargains

If you would like to bring back home some delectable packets of pure cane sugar or pots of local coffee, do check out the northern towns where you can actually buy sugar directly from factories. South Kona, on the other hand, is a town that is fiercely proud of Hawaii's coffee heritage and offers several coffee-themed gift packs that can serve as excellent souvenirs. More importantly, the prices are quite affordable.

Whenever I pass through Hawaii, I always like to pick up some kind of craft as a souvenir. One of my favorite places to pick up souvenirs is in Hawi, at the L Zeidman Gallery. This particular establishment specializes in handcrafted sculptures and bowls that are actually made from no less than 50 different types of local wood. The prices are admittedly on the steeper side, but if you ask me, it's entirely worth it. If you're looking for traditional sarongs in bright colors, Hawaiian dresses, handbags and other such accessories, you can also check out Sig Zane department store.

For a more unique shopping experience, head over to Honolulu where you can attend the Aloha Stadium Swap Meet. This event is held several times per week and doesn't involve any money so be sure to take along anything you would like to swap with the other swappers.

Traditional Hawaiian souvenirs that you'll love

Some of the things that I just can't leave Hawaii without include:

Hawaiian jewelry

Especially pearls that are harvested right in front of you at Maui's famous Diver's Jewelry store. Do check out the bracelets, charms and pendants that bear local symbols such as flip-flops, sea turtles, tropical flowers, shells and the likes.

Clothes in Hawaiian print

Created in the 1930's by tailors based in Honolulu, Hawaiian shirts have vastly soared in popularity since then and I always make it a must to get a shirt or a dress in the flowery prints that helped put Hawaii on the map. Along with shirts, you can also find bikinis, sarongs, hats, flip flops and tops in the same print. Another must-have Aloha wear is, of course, the grass skirt. Whether you plan on wearing it or not, the skirt

A nice packet of Chinese seeds

This is something else that I absolutely must pick up in Hawaii. Yes I know, you didn't go to the Big Island to pick up seeds from China, but contrary to what you may believe, these seeds are locally grown. These seeds actually first arrived on the island back in the 19th century with Chinese migrant workers and have now become an integral part of Hawaiian culture. In some strip malls, you might also find shops with jars filled with dried fruit seeds such as crack seed, pickled mango, salted lemon, salt plum, li hing mui and many more. These also have the advantage of being quite lightweight which will make it easier for you to pack.

The world highest-grade coconut oils

We all know that coconut oil is excellent for the skin but did you know that Hawaii has one of the highest-grade coconut oils in the world? More importantly, the prices also have the advantage of being quite affordable so it might pay off to stock up. This oil can also be used in the kitchen: I personally love to drizzle it over hot popcorn for a delicious albeit healthy snack. Do remember to pack the oil in your checked luggage though, because most airlines do have liquid restrictions and you wouldn't want your purchases to get confiscated at the airport.

Hawaiian-related scents and flavors

While you're on a roll with the coconut oil and all, you can also check out the numerous other products that pack various Hawaiian-related scents and flavors, such as shampoos, shower gels, body butters and the likes. Other examples include incense sticks and scented candles. When you're back home and feeling nostalgic about your holiday under the sun, one whiff at these types of products will transport you right back to Hawaii and the neighboring islands.

Conclusion

Bottom line is: If you want to visit Hawaii, go for it. Regardless of what your budget is, Hawaii is such a diverse country with so much to do that you will undoubtedly find something that matches your financial limitations, both in terms of accommodation and entertainment.

Don't forget to read up as much as you can prior to your trip and compare different packages to ensure that you get a good deal. When booking a trip to Hawaii (or anywhere in the world, really), don't forget that the rule of the thumb is: if it sounds too good to be true, it's definitely is so be smart and avoid potential traps.

Once you're there, take a second to just close

your eyes and take a deep breath. Enjoy the scent of fresh plumeria as it fuses gloriously with the salt-tinged sea breeze as you bury your toes into the warm, silky sand. Later that day, be sure to book a hike towards a hidden waterfall where you can dip into the exceptionally refreshing waters before heading back to your hotel for an invigorating full-body scrub. Later that evening, just sit by the shore and sip on your favorite drink as you enjoy one of the most beautiful sunsets in the world.

Yep- that's Hawaii for you.

Thank you so much for reading the book. I hope it's useful for you.

If you like the book, would you please do me a huge favor and write me a review on Amazon? I would really appreciate it and look forward to reading your review.

Best

Thomas

45889533R00057

Made in the USA
Middletown, DE
16 July 2017